RICHMOND
EST 1885

THE PICTORIAL STORY OF RICHMOND'S 2017 AFL PREMIERSHIP

TIGER TIME

Introduction by Peggy O'Neal
Photos courtesy of AFL Media
Words by Russell Jackson

www.slatterymedia.com

INKED INTO HISTORY: It was a sight many Richmond supporters feared never witnessing again, but the Premiership Cup was finally in their keeping by the end of 2017—due in no small part to their brilliant midfield, led by skipper Trent Cotchin and superstar Dustin Martin.

TIGER TIME

SING WHILE YOU'RE WINNING: Skipper Trent Cotchin, Brownlow medal-winning star Dustin Martin and spearhead Jack Riewoldt had all endured lean times at Tigerland. Riewoldt, in particular, showed his emotions on-field when the siren sounded. None was afraid to put a little extra oomph into the team song, as Grand Final destiny awaited the men in yellow and black.

CONTENTS

INTRODUCTION 8
Club President Peggy O'Neal reflects on a remarkable achievement.

THE ROAD AHEAD 10
The long journey to a Premiership begins on the sweltering Sunshine Coast.

THE TIGER RENAISSANCE 24
Damien Hardwick's reborn side takes the AFL by surprise.

DESTINY BECKONS 58
The Tigers overcome their finals hoodoo in emphatic style.

DREAMS BECOME REALITY 88
The thrilling finale to a season in which the Tigers said, 'Why not us?'

PREMIERS 138
A 37-year drought come to an end.

PARTY TIME 174

UNITY PREVAILS

Season 2017 was remarkable for the Richmond Football Club for many reasons, not the least of which was winning our 11th Premiership—as illustrated so beautifully in this book.

Was the Premiership against the odds, as many have suggested? Well, no team has ever come from finishing 13th one season to winning a Premiership the next. But did we ever think that the odds were against us? If you think about odds too much, if you let any doubt compromise your confidence that you can achieve your goal, you probably won't make it.

I don't think Damien Hardwick was thinking about the odds being against us when he constructed a team that played (and won) a Finals series with one traditional ruckman and one traditional forward, nor when he examined himself to determine the kind of coach he needed to be in order to build a team that showed a spirit and endeavour that could not be broken, but that could (and would) break others. The Richmond team of 2017 played in the image of the coach.

I don't think Dustin Martin was thinking about odds when he put together a season which broke all individual records. He became the most decorated player in history (I suspect he was always thinking about how he could make the team better), and then made the monumental decision to remain a Tiger for life.

I don't think Brendon Gale was thinking about odds as he applied himself every day in 2017 (and the previous seven years of his tenure as CEO) to guide the Club to be the best that it could be, when he made it a personal mission to build a financial and cultural platform that would allow the team to succeed, and that would make the Club an organisation of which all Tigers could be proud.

I don't think Trent Cotchin ever thought about odds when he considered how he could become the captain that the team needed—discovering that his true self was what we needed, and that within that true self was a Premiership captain who connected with his teammates in an unprecedented way.

I don't think Jack Graham was considering the odds of a teenager making a difference in the Club's most important game of the last 37 years when, with four minutes left in the second quarter, he kicked the goal which put us ahead. We never trailed again. It seemed to me that he was just relishing the challenge, as were the rest of the team.

I don't think that Alex Rance or Jack Riewoldt considered the odds when they took responsibility as vice-captains and went about organising and guiding the back line and forward line, respectively, and carried out the coach's game plan to turn their teammates into pressure machines.

When I am asked for one reason that made this season different—one reason that the odds didn't matter—I would have to say unity: a singular vision that the right path was in front of us and that the right people were in place to do the job.

That unity was demonstrated in the character of staff and players, and in the strength of purpose that provided a beacon to all of us as the Club went about its business every day. It was demonstrated in the revelation that playing the game at any age should continue to contain that important element of 'play', and that work can be both fulfilling and fun when you are working with people whom you care about, and who care about you.

And, of course, unity is most evident in the support given to the Club year after year by the Tiger Army and all our volunteers. The Premiership belongs to our supporters: they are the reason that the Club exists and they are the reason we play the game.

Success like this only comes to united football Clubs and we now have our evidence that a united Club is a powerful force; in fact, unity has made us a strong and bold Premiership Club.

Finally, now that a little time has passed, I am sure all Richmond supporters have reflected on the magnitude of what happened on 30 September and asked themselves: how did this team do it and why now?

I would say that the correct questions were: why not us, and why not now? We answered both questions most emphatically.

We didn't think about the odds.

Peggy O'Neal

**PEGGY O'NEAL,
PRESIDENT, RICHMOND FOOTBALL CLUB
OCTOBER 2017**

MISSION ACCOMPLISHED: Peggy O'Neal and Brendon Gale weathered as much criticism as the players and coaches along the path to Premiership glory, but Richmond's Grand Final triumph vindicated their calm and dignified leadership.

THE ROAD AHEAD

The best thing that could be said about Richmond's prospects heading into season 2017 was that it was unburdened by lofty expectations. Following a 13th place finish in 2016—cemented by an embarrassing 113-point loss in the final round—yet more calls came for coach Damien Hardwick's head. Agitators circled, restlessness formed, but Richmond president Peggy O'Neal, CEO Brendon Gale and the entire Board stood firm: it was time to reboot, not start again.

Having farewelled the experienced trio of Brett Deledio, Troy Chaplin and Ty Vickery, Richmond's unknown quantity in the off-season was precisely what their new faces would bring to the table. Much was expected of high-profile midfield recruit Dion Prestia. Josh Caddy would also bring plenty of midfield experience to bear, lightening the load on Trent Cotchin and Dustin Martin, and former Sydney ruckman Toby Nankervis seemed a canny addition. Yet to make their debuts were the likes of Dan Butler, Shai Bolton, Tyson Stengle, and Jack Graham. Would Richmond need to gamble on youth? What did their best 22 even look like?

Revamped also was Richmond's coaching panel, after seven key personnel changes. Back to the fold came former Lions coach Justin Leppitsch, who'd been one of Hardwick's deputies between 2009 and 2013, and highly regarded Blake Caracella, who'd spent seven successful years with Geelong. Former Crow Ben Rutten switched to the important role of backline coach. Fourth-year development coach Andrew McQualter took on midfield stoppages. Hardwick holidayed a little longer than usual, relaxing and recharging. New faces, different voices, fresh ideas. By the time Richmond's pre-season training trip to the Sunshine Coast was done, the entire atmosphere within Tigerland had transformed.

Fortuitously, the selection committee had 43 fit men to choose from by round one. "The magnets have been flying around non-stop. It's a great place to be," Hardwick said before his side faced the Blues. His optimism was mirrored by Trent Cotchin. "We're talking about reinvigoration, excitement and positivity," the captain said. Ever so slowly, the mood at Punt Road Oval was lightening, and a new Tiger spirit was emerging from the ashes of 2016.

SUMMER HOLIDAY: In the summer months, when sandy beaches seemed more appealing, Richmond players like Kane Lambert and Brandon Ellis were pounding the pavement and preparing themselves for a gruelling AFL season. In January, the Tigers ventured to the Sunshine Coast for a pre-season training camp, and there was rarely any shade in which to rest or hide.

THE ROAD AHEAD

LISTEN UP: Coach Damien Hardwick resolved to embrace his inner comedian during the 2017 campaign, and even went away on an extended holiday during the off-season break to freshen up for the challenges ahead. He was soon back to the serious business of drilling his men once January arrived.

TRUE GRIT: Brandon Ellis is among Richmond's toughest and most durable players, and had not missed a single senior game in the four seasons leading into 2017. During weights sessions he is a study in gut-busting effort, pushing himself to the brink of exhaustion.

WRESTLEMANIA: At one point Richmond's training camp resembled an episode of It's a Knockout. Tiger defenders Nathan Broad and David Astbury weren't giving their boss an inch when the water activities became physical. Both would prove the worth of their exertions once the season reached its remarkable conclusion.

FLIPPING OUT: Tigers mainstay Kamdyn McIntosh is a pacey linebreaker with a Sherrin in his hands, but in downtime during Richmond's northern excursion, he took the opportunity to indulge in more acrobatic endeavours.

MIND OVER MATTER: His stingy defending efforts and stern-faced demeanour on the football field might give the impression Alex Rance takes everything in life so seriously, but he is one of the great pranksters of the Richmond squad. Always ready with a quip, and often lightening the mood in tough times, he's been an invaluable member of the club's leadership group, alongside Trent Cotchin and Jack Riewoldt.

GREAT EXPECTATIONS: Looking shy and reserved on the training track once the Tigers started 'ball work', teenage recruit Jack Graham could never have foreseen what was in store for him during his first AFL season. Picked up at number 53 in the national draft, after Adelaide and Port Adelaide each passed him by on multiple occasions, the South Australian's name would be on the lips of every football fan in the country by late September.

THOUSAND YARD STARE: There was no slackening for Tigers players on the Australia Day public holiday. Daniel Rioli's look of fierce focus would eventually provide an apt metaphor for Richmond's efforts in season 2017. Rioli's evolution to match-winning star was one of the stories of the season. After his four goals in the Preliminary Final, he shared best afield honours with Dustin Martin in the Coaches' award.

MEET AND GREET: Before an intra-club practice match in Maroochydore, Tigers spearhead Jack Riewoldt provided young fan Finley Coll with a happy memory of Richmond's Sunshine Coast trip, stopping by for a pre-game chat. Often the public face of the playing group as a TV regular on FoxFooty's AFL 360, Riewoldt is a bundle of energy and fun.

GAMES BEGIN: Richmond's JLT Community Series fixtures took them to locations as far-flung as Moe and Mount Gambier, where Dylan Grimes can be seen getting his kick away in the Tigers' 28-point victory against Port Adelaide. The Tigers suffered a seven-point loss against the Pies to finish their tune-ups, but had previously opened their 2017 practice match account with a victory against an opponent of then-unknown significance: Adelaide.

TIGER TIME

THE TIGER RENAISSANCE

The Tigers burst out of the blocks in the first month of the season proper, catching the competition by surprise with their fleet of small, speedy forwards buzzing around at full-forward Jack Riewoldt's feet. In round one, the annual season-opener against Carlton, second-year youngsters Daniel Rioli, Jason Castagna and debutant Dan Butler kicked six goals between them. It gave fans an early glimpse of what was possible when Richmond applied such relentless pressure to opposition defences. It also hinted at the duality these reborn Tigers would show in 2017; defenders who took risks and played positively, forwards who defended determinedly when they weren't capitalising on the hard work of their teammates up the field.

Of course, the words 'pressure' and 'Richmond' became synonymous as a means of easily explaining the Tiger renaissance, but other factors were at play during the home and away season. Being able to call upon the best midfielder and defender in the competition—especially ones hitting their respective primes—certainly didn't hurt, for one. Hardwick's men were also clear-headed and creative, took risks in the name of positivity, and held true to their pre-season promise of showing their affection for one another when things went well. It was an instinctive and attractive style of play, carried out by footballers who trusted each other.

Stern challenges came. A four-game losing streak between rounds six and nine—including back-to-back heartbreakers against Fremantle and GWS—prompted a fresh round of schadenfreude among opposition barrackers. Emerging from that rut, the Tigers would not drop consecutive games for the rest of the season, nor would they lose twice to the same opponent. A welcome headache developed, too: heart and soul players like Steven Morris, Anthony Miles and Taylor Hunt were no longer guaranteed a game. Healthy competition for spots kept the starting line-up humming.

Still, by the end of the home and away season, what lay ahead was not entirely clear. Rousing interstate wins in Perth, Adelaide (against the Power) and the Gold Coast—plus a late-season triumph at home over Premiership fancies GWS—showed the Tigers were not just flat-track bullies. What nagged away in the minds of doubters was how they'd fared against other top sides. Adelaide had soundly thumped them. Sydney and Geelong both edged the Tigers out in tight games. Could Hardwick's men withstand those sides in September? Nothing in the club's recent past suggested so, but some major surprises were in store.

GAME PLAN: After eight headline-making years at the helm, Tigers coach Damien Hardwick rewarded the club's faith, leading his team through an inspired campaign of irresistible football. The strategy was to encourage a potent combination of defensive pressure, creative license and fun. He became the first coach to lift a side from lower than 12th place the previous season to the Premiership dais. The Tigers went from the outhouse to the penthouse in 2017.

FLYING HIGH: For the fourth successive occasion the two sides had met in round one, the Tigers opened their home and away account in grand style, thumping Carlton by 43 points in the season-opener at the MCG. Dustin Martin's 33 possessions and four goals were an ominous sign of things to come, while Daniel Rioli and his 'Mosquito fleet' partners Jason Castagna and Dan Butler managed six majors between them. Rioli soared into the night to kick-start a spectacular season

THE FLYING RUCKMAN: Injuries would hamper the season of popular Tiger Ben Griffiths, but he flew high for a spectacular mark in Richmond's round two win over the Pies. His future clouded by a series of concussions, Griffiths was able to return to action during the finals run of the club's VFL side.

BALL: Among the new arrivals at Tigerland for season 2017, Josh Caddy was making his presence felt from day one. This tackle on Collingwood's Henry Schade typified Richmond's ferocious attack on the contest in the early stages of the season, and indeed Caddy's. The former Gold Coast Suns and Geelong midfielder reinvented himself at his third AFL home, mixing time in the midfield with spells up forward, as required. He finished the season with 21 goals, including a career-high four against Hawthorn in round 20.

TIGER TIME

GOAL OF THE YEAR: The Tigers maintained their perfect start to the season against West Coast in round three, and it was due in no small part to the heroics of Daniel Rioli. Most memorably, he jinked, jumped, baulked and weaved his way free before curling a majestic checkside goal from the pocket at the Punt Road end. Twice he'd brought the ball to ground in contests ahead of the scoring opportunity. That compelling mix of hard work, defensive pressure and sublime skill was his benchmark in 2017. On Brownlow night, this effort was rubber-stamped as the official goal of the season.

DOWNWARD MOMENTUM: A dizzying early-season run of five straight wins came crashing down in the month following, when Richmond dropped four games in a row. The last of those, in round nine, was a heartbreaking three-point failure against GWS. The Giants went coast-to-coast with a minute left on the clock, and their superstar forward Jeremy Cameron sunk the Tigers with a long bomb through the middle. Naysayers circled their wagons, but that gutting defeat would prove to be the last time Richmond lost consecutive games for the rest of 2017. From their lowest ebb, they emerged with renewed focus and clarity of purpose.

TIGER TIME

DREAMTIME AT THE 'G: Some 85,656 fans poured through the gates for Richmond's Indigenous Round clash with Essendon—a League record attendance for a Saturday night game—and the Tiger Army was rewarded with a rousing 15-point win. Indigenous stars Shane Edwards and Daniel Rioli helped Shai Bolton (centre) to his maiden victory in the yellow and black, but it was another new face—former Swans ruckman Toby Nankervis—who kicked the sealer.

THE TIGER RENAISSANCE

LEFT IN THE DUST: By the end of the season it was easy to see why North Melbourne was keen on luring Dustin Martin away from Punt Road. In round 11 Brad Scott's men got a first-hand glimpse of his brilliance when the star on-baller's 38 possessions and two goals laid waste to the Kangaroos. That 35-point triumph had the Tigers back inside the top four. Months on, with Martin's new contract finally inked, teammate Brandon Ellis turned up for Mad Monday festivities dressed as Dusty the Kangaroo. Ellis could afford to laugh: by then Martin was a Richmond player for life.

TRIAL AND RETRIBUTION: A comfortable 26-point victory over Carlton in round 14 was marred by an incident in which running defender Bachar Houli concussed Carlton's Jed Lamb in a clumsy attempt at breaking away from the Blues tagger. After hearing character references from sources including Prime Minister Malcolm Turnbull and TV host Waleed Aly, the AFL Tribunal initially handed down a two-week suspension, but an unprecedented appeal by the AFL ended with a four-week sanction for a contrite Houli. The resultant media attention had the potential to destabilise Tiger efforts, but they blocked out the noise and their star backman returned to his dashing best against Gold Coast in round 19.

SUPPORTING CAST: The '19th man' factor was never stronger for the Tigers than in 2017, a year in which they'd finish with more than 75,000 members. Renowned as the loudest supporters in the League, they're also among the most loyal. They stuck with the club through that long period in the wilderness after 1982, the club's last Grand Final appearance.

STAND ASIDE: Proving they were not just flat-track bullies on the MCG, the Tigers travelled to the fortress of Adelaide Oval in round 15 and returned with the four points. To pull that off they needed to charge home in a 13-point win over Port Adelaide. Dustin Martin's fend-off of Power star Hamish Hartlett spoke of a newfound ruthlessness to Tiger efforts. In what proved a three-vote Brownlow medal performance, Martin amasssed 36 disposals and a goal.

FLASH AND DASH: In that low-scoring game against the Power, each of Daniel Butler's three goals were precious commodities. By the midway point of his maiden season in senior ranks, the small forward had become—along with Daniel Rioli and Jason Castagna—a vital component of Damien Hardwick's forward structure. Butler's goals and score assists were one thing, but it was his relentless chasing and tackling that gave opposition defences second thoughts.

THE TIGER RENAISSANCE

FIGHT LIKE MADDIE: Richmond and St Kilda's round 16 clash at Etihad stadium was staged again as 'Maddie's Match', in honour of Jack Riewoldt's late cousin. In what proved his final season in League ranks, Maddie's brother Nick and his Saints teammates took the honours in a thumping 67-point win—a worrying capitulation from the Tigers. In this instance, important funds raised for research into bone marrow failure syndrome put the result in perspective.

THE TIGER RENAISSANCE

ROYAL RUMBLE: The scoreboard in Richmond's 31-point win over Brisbane in Round 17 suggested a regulation win, but there was plenty of niggle and spite at Etihad Stadium. Mild-mannered defender David Astbury stepped in and dealt with Lions midfield pest Rhys Mathieson when the contest reached its most willing.

OUTMUSCLED: In a sign of things to come, Richmond out-bodied and then outlasted the Giants in round 18, prevailing by 19 points at a waterlogged MCG. Alex Rance made his presence felt around mercurial Giant Steve Johnson, who failed to hit the scoreboard in a low-scoring slog.

RAIN DANCE: Jack Riewoldt persevered in difficult conditions to finish the day as the only multiple goal-kicker against the Giants. That win put Richmond back inside the top four again—a position in which they'd hold firm for the rest of the home and away season. They'd been burnt in the past, but the Tigerland faithful were beginning to wonder whether this delightfully unpredictable 2017 Premiership race was open to a Richmond raid.

THE SUN ALWAYS RISES: After round 19, Geelong star Patrick Dangerfield found himself ineligible for the Brownlow Medal, clearing the way for Dustin Martin to become a short-priced favourite. More pressing for Richmond was the task of accounting for Gold Coast, which they did to the tune of 33 points at Carrara. This gang tackle on Suns midfielder Michael Rischitelli hints at the discrepancy in the tackle count. In years gone by this would have been a danger game for the Tigers, but they got the job done with minimal fuss.

CAPTAIN FANTASTIC: One of the goals Trent Cotchin set himself before the 2017 season was to do anything within his power to ensure Dustin Martin produced a Brownlow medal-winning season, even if it meant sacrificing his own game. The 2012 co-winner of football's highest honour was no slouch himself. He gathered 29 possessions to dominate his side's 29-point round 20 victory against Hawthorn. Not long ago the Hawks were the competition benchmark, and Luke Hodge the AFL's most revered captain. Now the Tigers were on the march, and Cotchin had become a respected leader in the Hodge tradition.

THE TIGER RENAISSANCE

A HARD ROAD: For all Richmond's progress in 2017, doubts as to their genuine Premiership credentials lingered after a tight away loss to Geelong in round 21. Fill-in Cats full-forward Harry Taylor punished the Tigers, and full-back Alex Rance, with four goals, but there were also encouraging signs in the third quarter, when the Tigers trimmed three goals off the home side's lead to stay in touch. If nothing else it was an insight into the tune-ups Richmond required to compete with the best.

SUBI SLAUGHTER: Proving that travelling west no longer held any fear, the Tigers thumped Fremantle by 104 points to boost their percentage and find peak form at the right time of the season. Amid a goal avalanche at Subiaco—in the last AFL match to be held at the famous ground—the story of the afternoon was Jacob Townsend's six majors in his first senior game of 2017. Drafted into the side as a defensive forward, the former GWS midfielder provided a late-season spark and introduced an element of surprise that opposition defences hadn't predicted.

COMING HOME STRONGLY: Eager to reach September with a full wind in their sails, the Tigers showed no sympathy for the Saints in Nick Riewoldt's farewell to League football, cruising to a 41-point win at the MCG. Jacob Townsend had another field day with five goals, and there were three each for Jack Riewoldt and Shaun Grigg. Again, Dustin Martin did as he pleased with 36 possessions and two goals, one of them a jaw-dropping checkside that had Tiger fans hugging each other in the aisles. At the end of a fascinating final round, the Tigers had locked in third place and a double chance in September. Momentum was building and the Tigers had also secured an effective "home" final, against second-placed Geelong.

THE TIGER RENAISSANCE

THE JOB AHEAD: Coach Damien Hardwick had led his recalibrated side to a third-place finish, only half a game behind the ladder leaders. He had done so with a side that finished 13th the previous year, and in pre-season discussions barely figured in the hypothetical top eights among the game's pundits. But why not the Tigers, Hardwick wondered. A year earlier the Bulldogs had shocked the football world. Maybe it really was Tiger Time.

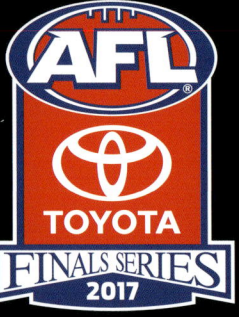

DESTINY BECKONS

As finals eve drew close, many within Tiger Army ranks would have cast their minds back to the corresponding month of 2013. At that point, having finished the regular season in fifth position—qualifying for Richmond's first finals campaign in 12 often harrowing years—the Tigers were on clover. Against default finalists Carlton, vaulted into the Premiership race by Essendon's suspension, Hardwick's resurgent side led by four goals at half-time, seemingly revelling in the volcanic atmosphere. The margin might have been even healthier. Seldom had a week one finals crowd barracked louder.

Then it happened—the inevitable. In front of 94,690 howling fans the Tigers fell in a heap, losing their once handsome lead and then the game. It was devastating and utterly predictable in equal measure, at least given their recent history. Slowly they moved on. A year later they scraped into September with far less fanfare, to face Port Adelaide away. It hurt no less when they were trounced. Another season wasted. In 2015 it was another eighth-placed side—North Melbourne—that ran down the Tigers from behind. A giant anvil marked "Richmond" kept plummeting from the sky. Fatalism had set about its work. This was becoming worse than the "Ninth-mond" jokes—another opportunity squandered.

In 2017 the Tigers had to overcome history, true, but also their sense of themselves. There was a surreal, counterintuitive bent to everything they did. It was not a slight of hand at work, rather a kind of football alchemy. In week one of the finals they drew Geelong, a football club steeped in success and the home to modern greats of the game—superior in most respects to Richmond's last three finals opponents. A side, then, that Richmond might fear.

Yet the Tigers calmly, methodically dismantled Chris Scott's side in an avalanche that took an hour to build and then landed spectacularly; the first half featured a combined total of five goals, in the second the Tigers piled on 10, to Geelong's three. Fifty-one points was the final margin. After 16 years without a finals win, Richmond had not only thrown off the shackles but inverted their reputation. They now had a week off in September. *That kind* of week off.

On preliminary final day, when the best laid plans of master coaches often go horribly awry, everything went exceedingly well. No slaves to reputation now, Hardwick's side took another hour-long look at a vaunted line-up—the young superstars of GWS—then simply blew them off the MCG. Again the Tigers had piled on ten goals in the second half, in which GWS managed only four. The worst pressure team in the league 12 months earlier, the Tigers had huffed and puffed and blown the house down. Grand Final destiny beckoned.

THIS WAY BOYS: Richmond's irresistible September run started with a 51-point demolition of early-season Premiership fancies Geelong, locking away a home Preliminary Final. Jack Riewoldt was his usual demonstrative self, but otherwise it was a tough night for tall forwards. The Tigers spread the load, with eleven individual goal-kickers as the Cats struggled to produce many scoring opportunities at all. The match was a replica of many through the season. After a tight first half, Richmond's pressure told, as the Tigers kicked ten goals to three in a dominant display.

TALL TIMBER: Toby Nankervis was edged out by Geelong's Zac Smith in the hit-out count, but with 20 possessions and plenty of valuable work around the ground, Richmond's ruckman was a vital contributor in his first finals game wearing the yellow and black.

GRUDGE MATCH: Former Cat Josh Caddy helped the Tigers brush aside his old team, taking team-lifting marks, winning plenty of contested ball and booting two goals in a star turn. By the end of the 2016 season, it was clear the underrated utility was no longer guaranteed a senior game at Geelong, nor a position in the midfield. At Tigerland he became a precious piece of the jigsaw puzzle.

SHUT IT DOWN: The bedrock of Richmond's performance against the Cats was a stingy defensive effort, and the concession of only five goals for the night. The ever-dependable David Astbury and Alex Rance were able to neutralise the threat of Geelong key forwards Tom Hawkins and Harry Taylor. Taylor had outpointed Rance a month earlier at Simonds Stadium, but Rance had learned his lesson well. He and Astbury kept Taylor to just one goal this time, and by then the game had slipped away for the Cats.

CATCH ME IF YOU CAN: Midfielder Shane Edwards showed Zach Guthrie a clean pair of heels during his sterling 24-possession game in the midfield. Edwards had to wait until his 205th League game and his 11th season to finally register a finals victory, but patience proved a virtue for the popular clubman.

PRIMAL SCREAM: The wait was also worthwhile for the dedicated Tiger Army, who drowned out a more subdued cohort of Geelong supporters. The concept of "the 19th man" had never been given more credence than when Richmond diehards latched onto momentum swings and raised their support to fever pitch. The vocal support for Richmond had Geelong officials wondering aloud whether Cats fans had had too much of a good thing, after competing in finals all but one season following their drought-breaking win in the 2007 decider.

UP AND AWAY: Kane Lambert and Brandon Ellis were two of the more unassuming heroes of Richmond's remarkable season. On Qualifying Final day Lambert lifted his game to a new level, helping himself to 24 possessions and a goal. It was another telling contribution to a Tigers win.

DESTINY BECKONS

LEADING BY EXAMPLE: When Trent Cotchin wasn't burrowing head-first into packs and winning 50-50 balls, he laid nine tackles in his side's breakthrough September victory. Never had the Tigers skipper been prouder to lead his team (L-R: Nick Vlastuin, Shaun Grigg, Josh Caddy, Nathan Broad, Toby Nankervis, Dustin Martin, David Astbury, Dylan Grimes and Brandon Ellis) down the MCG race and into the changerooms. Ahead of them was a week off, then a mouth-watering Preliminary Final matchup with Greater Western Sydney Giants.

ARMS RACE: Damien Hardwick, Trent Cotchin, Dustin Martin and Shaun Grigg were the old hands of Richmond's march through September, and the 'head of the snake' was an intimidating sight for any opponent in 2017. Here, on Preliminary Final day, Cotchin would once more lay nine tackles, paving the way for the more spectacular deeds of his teammates.

GOTCHA: Giants bellwether Toby Greene loomed as a danger man for the Tigers. Unwavering Richmond defender Dylan Grimes had other ideas, keeping the GWS star goalless in the Preliminary Final.

THE SPOILS: Giants forwards Toby Greene and Harrison Himmelberg had their work cut out for them thanks to David Astbury and his iron fist. Here the Tigers defender rises above the pack to repel another GWS forward entry.

WELL DONE MATE: Josh Caddy embraces Jason Castagna, the high-leaping dynamo who saved one of his best performances of the year for when it mattered dearly. Castagna's 18 possessions and a goal were instrumental to Richmond's forward structure, providing constant headaches for GWS defenders.

TIGER TIME

ONE LAST PUSH: The Preliminary Final finished as a contest when Richmond slammed on six goals to the Giants' one during the third term, setting up a 31-point lead at the final change. As they had done to Geelong in the Qualifying Final, the Tigers came out after the long break and smashed through their opponents. Regardless, Damien Hardwick was still cajoling his men into following their game plan until the final siren soared. Tim Livingston, Richmond's Head of Coaching and Football Performance, took his turn holding the magnet board

DESTINY BECKONS

FIERCE FOCUS: Early in Dustin Martin's career he was a housemate to his captain Trent Cotchin, and their close bond was evident as they came off the ground with a Grand Final appearance secured. Martin embraced coach Damien Hardwick and gave his skipper a knowing look: this was a job not yet finished.

HIGHER GROUND: No Tiger player had greater impact on the Preliminary Final outcome than small forward Daniel Rioli. In season 2017 the 20-year-old came of age, not just as an impact player capable of the occasional moment of individual brilliance, but a mature and consistent performer. His four goals was a career-high.

THE LID'S OFF: He became Richmond's youngest-ever Life Member before departing Tigerland at the end of the 2016 season, but Brett Deledio's first game against his old side proved a painful one. He'd suffered a number of injury setbacks in 2017—the story of recent seasons—but when he came into the GWS side for the first time in Round 20, Deledio looked to have timed his run perfectly. Alas, it wasn't to be for a favourite son of Punt Road Oval.

CREAM ON TOP: Dion Prestia's off-season arrival from Gold Coast was one of the most discussed player moves of 2017. Having struggled with consistency at the start of Richmond's campaign, he got better by the week and pieced together a strong finals campaign. Not only were his performances valuable in themselves, they lightened the load on Trent Cotchin and Dustin Martin—it was impossible for opposition midfielders to quell all three of them at once.

IVAN THE TERRIFIC: Plenty of fans were on hand at Etihad Stadium to send a beloved ruckman off in style, but cult hero Ivan Maric will not become a stranger to Tigerland. Maric played 77 games for Adelaide before crossing to Punt Road in 2012, and among his 157 League games were three finals appearances in the yellow and black.

TIGER TIME

HEARTBREAKER: Having made extraordinary progress under the tutelage of former Brisbane Premiership star Craig McCrae, Richmond's VFL side fell four points short of Premiership glory against Gary Ayres' Port Melbourne. Of the experienced hands, Ben Griffiths, Ben Lennon and Steven Morris were among those who went home empty-handed, and Lennon suffered the additional heartache of missing what would have been a match-winning shot at goal after the siren.

RECORD BREAKER: Dustin Martin's record-breaking tally of 36 votes, including a stunning 11 best-on-ground performances, made him a clear winner on Brownlow Medal night. "To everyone at the Richmond footy club, the coaches, the staff … what a week we've got in front of us," Martin said in his acceptance speech, one eye squarely fixed on Grand Final day. "I can't wait to finish it off with success this week."

DREAMS BECOME REALITY

Richmond's eleventh League Premiership came a testing 13,517 days since its last, and proved a triumph for the ages. It occurred not as the result of appointing some new coaching prophet, nor bringing back a club legend from the glory years of the 1960s and 70s. It was simply the destiny of a special group of players and a reborn coach—backed by a stable and clear-eyed team of administrators—all converging with a common purpose at precisely the right time.

The prideful Tigers of 2017 opened their hearts to each other. They didn't play like their lives depended on it; they galloped through the year with smiles on their faces, delighting in each other's success, heeding the refrain of their coaches: *have fun out there*. The key to turning Grand Final dreams into reality was achieving the fullest manifestation of their own carefully-constructed team ethos at the right time of year—September, the month that had haunted and stalked and outright mocked this football club for decades on end.

The naked facts are startling: Damien Hardwick's side catapulted itself from the ignominy of 13th place in 2016 to a 48-point demolition of the Premiership season's top side in the following year's decider. Premiership glory capped a delirious month in which the clogged arterial of Punt Road became Melbourne's most compelling thoroughfare of sporting successes. In addition to his Premiership medal, Dustin Martin took out the Brownlow, the Norm Smith and every other player-of-the-year award on offer. Hardwick was named coach of the year. Daniel Rioli pocketed goal of the year. If club CEO Brendon Gale had walked into any pub in the land and grabbed a raffle ticket, you fancy the meat tray

Hardwick's simple team mantra proved more and more apt as the season wore on: "Why not us?" Indeed, why not the team with the greatest and most physically intimidating midfielder in the competition? Why not the side with the League's best defender, and its most quietly determined captain? Why not the outfit with the most demonstrative key forward—bolstered by an irrepressible mosquito fleet, all feeding off unfailingly disciplined defence and a hard-nosed support cast of midfielders? Why not the football club with a fan base so loyal and loud they drowned out the mere *possibility* of negative thoughts? Why the hell not?

Still, the denouement exceeded all expectations. Adelaide got the jump and could have led by four goals at quarter time. Don Pyke's men had thrilled football fans all year, too. Yet the Tigers couldn't be denied. Little things became very big things; a rousing Alex Rance spoil; a Dustin Martin fend-off—an act now worthy of its own Champion Data category; Shane Edwards, Dion Prestia and Trent Cotchin winning the telling hard ball; Jacob Townsend barrelling into anything and anyone in his path; Bachar Houli's graceful barrage of clearing passes; teenager Jack Graham raining in goals. Pushed off their game by tiny, compounding increments, Adelaide soon fell into a chasm.

In the surreal, woozy aftermath, Richmond spirit animal Jack Riewoldt found himself on stage with Las Vegas rockers The Killers. He was recast as lead vocalist on their hit, Mr Brightside—originally released in 2004, when Richmond took out the wooden spoon and, well, you know the rest. "Coming out of my cage, and I've been doing just fine, Gotta gotta be down, Because I want it all," the song starts. That was then Tigers in 2017: not just out of their

FIST OF FURY: Josh Caddy was in the thick of the action all year for Richmond, and his flying start on Grand Final day was typical of those high-octane performances. Here he punches the ball clear of Adelaide's Jake Lever, who is given a helping hand by Jacob Townsend.

THUMBS UP: Shaun Grigg signals his approval to the Tigerland faithful. Punt Road Oval's grandstand was heaving with supporters during Richmond's last open training session before the Grand Final. Not all would secure a precious ticket, but the training ground filled with 16,000 diehard fans eager to watch on the big screen and enjoy the communal experience of success.

ROARSOME: He might have been a bundle of nerves inside, but coach Damien Hardwick continued to smile and joke as the gathered masses cheered Richmond's final training session of the season. His attention had turned to dismantling Adelaide's vaunted pack of forwards—Tex Walker, Eddie Betts, Charlie Cameron, Tom Lynch and Josh Jenkins.

DREAMS BECOME REALITY

POMP AND CEREMONY: The annual Grand Final parade to the MCG drew thousands of Tigers and Crows supporters into Melbourne's city centre. As it crept its way past the Old Treasury Building on Spring Street, Nick Vlastuin treated the crowd a sample of his beard-grooming routine

TIGER TIME

TRUE COLOURS: A few kicks away from Punt Road Oval, the Rowena Parade Corner Store and Café—where players are often seen getting their coffee fix—became the subject of pilgrimages by Tiger fans thanks to a Dustin Martin mural painted by graffiti artists Dvate and Danny Awes. All week, residents of the suburb formally known as Struggletown decked their houses and businesses out in black and yellow, getting behind the local team. Within a few days one local barber had queues out the door when fans started asking for Dustin Martin-style haircuts.

CALM BEFORE THE STORM: In the quiet morning hours before fans came streaming down the concourses and through the MCG gates to cheer their lungs out, an eerie silence fell over the arena. Some 100,021 patrons would soon fill the ground to capacity, creating an almighty racket inside Melbourne's sporting coliseum.

TIGER TIME

BANNER DAY:
Richmond's cheer squad hadn't needed to produce a Grand Final day banner idea for the best part of four decades, and threw back to some Tigers of old for inspiration.

STARTING LINE-UP: The on-ground team photo has only recently come back in vogue for the AFL Grand Final, and Richmond's players assembled for the club's first example since the 1943 decider.

Back row (L-R): Shane Edwards, Kane Lambert, Jason Castagna, Jacob Townsend, Nick Vlastuin, Alex Rance, Bachar Houli, David Astbury, Nathan Broad, Jack Graham, Toby Nankervis, Josh Caddy, Daniel Butler, Kamdyn McIntosh.

Front row (L-R): Dion Prestia, Dustin Martin, Dylan Grimes, Brandon Ellis, Damien Hardwick (coach), Trent Cotchin (captain), Jack Riewoldt, Shaun Grigg, Daniel Rioli.

TIGER TIME

OPENING BOUNCE: The traditional bounce of the ball has been under threat in recent seasons, but there is no sight and sound in football quite like it. On Grand Final day, Umpire Simon Meredith got proceedings off to the best possible start with a perfect bounce for Tigers ruckman Toby Nankervis and his Adelaide counterpart Sam Jacobs.

WRAPPED UP: The Tigers had to absorb Adelaide's early ascendancy and remain calm. Apprehending Rory Laird in unison, Dion Prestia and Jacob Townsend typified the Tigers' clear focus on tackling pressure and nailing the basics.

DREAMS BECOME REALITY

READY TO POUNCE: Alex Rance marshalled his defensive colleagues perfectly throughout the 2017 campaign. Grand Final day was no different, even when Adelaide maintained a two-goal advantage in the early stages of the game.

TIGER TIME

CADDY STACK: Perhaps Richmond's most underrated off-season arrival, Josh Caddy opened the Tigers' goal-scoring account on Grand Final day, after Adelaide had dominated early, with goals to Rory Sloane and Eddie Betts in the first five minutes. A versatile player, Caddy's strong marking, scoring capacity and chest-puffing aggression brought as much to Richmond's compelling mix of talent and desire as any new face of 2017. All season long he made an impact in whatever role he was assigned, including that of tall marking option inside 50. Soon it became hard to believe that any club was ever willing to part with him, as both Gold Coast and Geelong had done.

FEAR THE BEARD: Like Richmond's season, Nick Vlastuin's Viking beard grew stronger and more intimidating as 2017 wore on. The flint-hard defender and occasional inside midfielder endured an early Grand Final blunder when an uncharacteristic fumble gifted Eddie Betts a goal, but he regained his composure quickly. All day he marked and spoiled strongly, rebounding to great effect in a typically understated performance. "Thanks to the boys for helping us get up, so I don't have to think about that for the rest of my life," Vlastuin joked afterwards.

BROAD SWORD: The hallmark of Nathan Broad's late-season emergence was his selfless running and regular performance of one-percenters—traits displayed again in a disciplined Grand Final effort. This time it was Adelaide's dangerous link man Tom Lynch who came off second best against the self-described fringe footballer, with Lynch forced further and further up the ground in order to get his hands on the ball. A one-time apprentice plumber from Western Australia's wheat belt region, Broad had played more reserves than seniors games for WAFL club Swan Districts when Richmond plucked him from obscurity as a mature-age recruit in 2015. He overcame a serious shoulder injury at the beginning of 2017—not to mention selection uncertainty—but calmly marked his place in Tiger history. Much of the pre-game focus was on Jack Graham's inexperience, but Broad triumphed in just his 11th game of AFL football.

DREAMS BECOME REALITY

LEADER OF THE PACK: Richmond's evolution from 13th-placed battlers to swaggering Premiers began at the top, with skipper Trent Cotchin emerging from the darkest period of his career and smiling more and more as season 2017 wore on. He poured his heart out to teammates in the off-season, and they responded by forming deeper personal connections with each other than Cotchin said he had ever experienced. His most statistically impressive individual performances came in the first two finals, but on Grand Final day Cotchin was tough in the clinches, typically brave, and in lifting the Premiership Cup banished 37 years of suffering and pain. The 2012 Brownlow Medallist once said he'd retire if he led the Tigers to a flag. He might be revising that ultimatum now.

JACK IN THE BOX: So often players who miss a succession of early scoring chances in Grand Finals serve as an unfortunate barometer of losing sides. Tigers spearhead Jack Riewoldt recovered well from three such misses and did the opposite, contesting fiercely for marks and running down Rory Laird from behind. Later Riewoldt kicked two majors to set his side on the path to victory. The first of those, a 40-metre snap across his body at the beginning of the second term, started a seven-goal run for the Tigers. He finished with 54 goals for the season, passing the half-century mark for eighth time in his last nine campaigns. His performances are as reliable as his displays of passion.

THE ICE MAN: Defensive forward Jacob Townsend came from nowhere late in 2017, booting 13 goals with his first 21 kicks of the season after returning to the side in Round 22. That output slowed a little in September, but in addition to two crucial Grand Final goals, the former GWS midfielder limited the aerial influence of Crows defender Jake Lever. Undaunted by his big moment, Townsend roughed up all of Lever, Josh Jenkins and, most memorably, Crows midfield star Matt Crouch, who was buried in a fierce tackle to lift Tiger spirits. Moments later, outnumbered two to one, Townsend contested with similar determination to win a free kick within scoring range and coolly converted the set shot. Add his goal from a kick-in intercept and Townsend was truly influential, and a key man in snuffing out Adelaide hopes.

THE ROCK: Having taken GWS linchpin Toby Greene out of the contest in Richmond's Preliminary Final victory, defensive stalwart Dylan Grimes pulled off a second coup in as many weeks by limiting the impact of Crows champion Eddie Betts. The Adelaide livewire had just seven disposals and a single goal to his name by the final siren. Grimes used to fear the noise of large crowds. This time around he silenced the Adelaide supporters with a commanding performance against one of the game's greatest forwards—a typically crucial role in his side's success. At the Richmond presentation night, Grimes won the inaugural Francis Bourke award—voted on weekly by his peers—as the team member who best upheld Richmond's trademark values of awareness, unity, relentlessness and discipline.

RICHMOND ROYALTY: Preliminary Final hero Daniel Rioli provided his usual manic pressure inside Richmond's attacking zone, but couldn't match his scoring efforts of a week earlier in the decider. A slip of a thing when he arrived on the AFL stage 18 months earlier, Rioli's astonishing rise to become one of the most damaging defensive forwards in the game was a telling factor in the tale. His coach, with whom Rioli has boarded for his first two AFL seasons, may never want him to move out of the Hardwick home. A family football tradition of achieving greatness on Grand Final day gathers more lustre by the year. Daniel's uncle Maurice won the Norm Smith Medal in Richmond's 1982 loss to Carlton, and his cousin Cyril is a four-time Premiership player for Hawthorn, and the 2015 Norm Smith Medallist

TITCH FIBRE: Quiet-achieving Shane Edwards is beloved of the Tiger faithful for exactly the kind of hard-nosed, unfussy role he played on Grand Final day. His 12 contested possessions, seven clearances and eight forward entries helped Richmond dominate stoppages and turn 50-50 contests into scoring opportunities. No doubt he was more than content with helping turn his 207th League game into the party to end all parties. Equally adept at creating and defending, Edwards was another Tiger who thrived when the heat was still in the contest, confirming himself as a big-game performer.

NANK THE TANK: A low-key pickup before the 2017 campaign, Toby Nankervis rose from the relative obscurity of being Shaun Hampson's understudy to a telling performer on the grandest stage. Well beaten by Adelaide colossus Sam Jacobs in the first half, Nankervis surged in the second, finishing with 18 possessions, 28 hit-outs and five telling forward entries. His ground work was superb for a big man. Adelaide seemed to view him as a weak link early in the game but he responded emphatically. Nankervis, who came to the Tigers for Pick 45 in the 2016 Draft, took more intercept marks than any ruckman in the competition in 2017, forever dropping back into defensive positions and making his presence felt. He also tripled his career games tally as one of the recruits of the season, and Tiger fans will be looking for more of the same from the 23-year-old in 2018.

HARD BALL: Regardless of the outcome in the ruck contests, Dion Prestia and his midfield colleagues won the lion's share of the hard ball. By the end of the day Richmond had outmuscled Adelaide's on-ballers, ending in a contested possession differential of 30. They edged the Crows in the clearances and stoppages too.

TIGER TIME

SIR RANCE-A LOT: The best defender in the League was simply dominant in the first half. When the game was up for grabs, he was a major factor in Richmond keeping Adelaide goalless for an entire quarter for the first time in the clubs' 27-year rivalry. Ten intercepts demoralised his opponents. Among the momentum altering acts early in the game, when Adelaide led by two goals, none was more resounding than Rance's iron first to repel a low pass heading onto Tex Walker's chest. That set the tone for a commanding defensive effort in which Richmond answered the critics who said they'd struggle to contain the League's most imposing collection of forwards. Alex Rance almost walked away from the game in 2015. Now he owns a most stylish piece of neckwear to go with all those All-Australian blazers. Named All-Australian captain, Rance finished second to Dustin Martin in the Jack Dyer Medal.

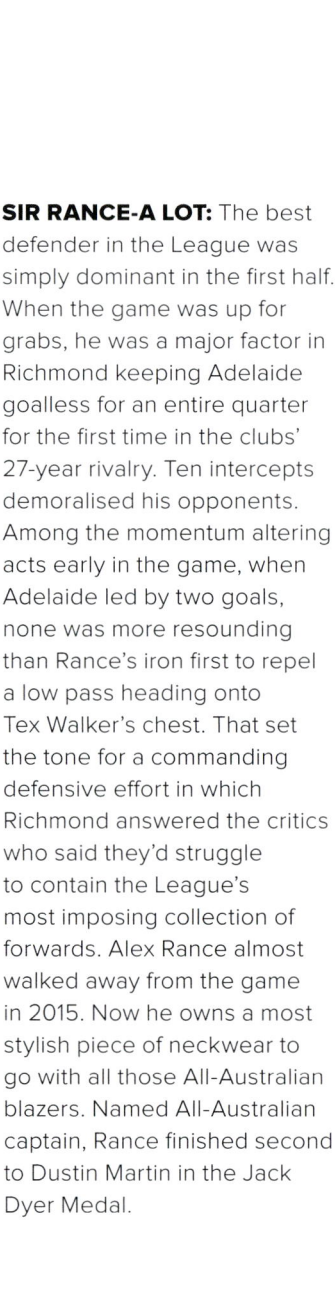

THE BOLTER: Jack Graham showed no signs of youthful nerves on Grand Final day, and the only teenager on the ground finished just his fifth League appearance in Norm Smith Medal contention. Sixteen possessions, five clearances and three crucial goals added to his remarkably composed efforts while also limiting the impact of Adelaide ball magnet Rory Sloane—Graham's childhood hero. "I was like, 'Hell, I'm going to be running with my idol here'," Graham thought to himself when coaches tapped him on the shoulder. Sloane had only a handful of disposals thereafter. Graham's goals put Richmond four, 15 and 26 points up, respectively. Each was a dagger in Adelaide hearts. Having played SANFL football for North Adelaide in 2016, Graham was passed over three times by the Crows on draft day. Now he's the seventh youngest Premiership star in Tiger history—only Bill James (1920) and Jack Anderson (1932) had played fewer games for a Richmond flag

DON'T ARGUE: As a youngster, Dustin Martin would play footy well into the night on his own field, one mowed into a paddock on the family's one-hectare farm in Castlemaine. On Grand Final day the midfield superstar played like he owned the MCG too, racking up an eye-popping 22 contested possessions in his 29 touches. He also slammed home two spirit-lifting goals. The second of those put Richmond 53 points clear amid a deafening din. Nobody since fellow country boy Tony Lockett has kicked more majors in a Brownlow-winning season. Martin finished the season with 37, a career high. "Start building the statue," ex-Tiger Rex Hunt said, and the Richmond faithful might just go ahead and do it now.

DREAMS BECOME REALITY

HOULI DOOLEY: Had each of Bachar Houli's three shots on goal sailed through the middle, he might have walked from the MCG with two medals around his neck. As it was, ten votes made him a clear second in Norm Smith Medal calculations, three votes astern of Dustin Martin. A selfless team player, Houli did almost as he pleased across half-back in a commanding display. The goal he did nail, in the first quarter, almost lifted the roof off the grandstand at the Punt Road end. His frequent intercepts and creativity were just as central to Richmond's triumph.

125

MIDFIELD PRESTIGE: Thriving in the void created by his higher-profile midfield colleagues, Dion Prestia capped a solid first year at Tigerland with a four-quarter Grand Final performance of relentless consistency. Twelve of his 27 possessions were contested (not quite the monstrous 19 he gathered in the Qualifying Final against Geelong), four drove Richmond into attack, and his final-quarter goal, a gift from Kane Lambert, put Richmond 45 points clear and kicked the MCG into party mode. When the ball needed to be won in the centre of the ground, Prestia was always in the thick of the contest. "We absolutely love each other and that just shows in the result," he said afterwards.

MAC ATTACK: Kamdyn McIntosh didn't offer as much of his trademark run and carry along the wing on Grand Final day, but the last Saturday in September rarely allows such freewheeling opportunities. McIntosh maintained his usual defensive pressure throughout the day and capped a consistent season by running, spreading, defending, and performing the kind of unglamorous one-percenters all winning teams require. Statistics were never going to measure his invaluable contribution to this side's winning balance. Like all the Tigers' Premiership heroes, he'll now delight in life membership of the Richmond Football Club—an initiative created halfway through 2017.

ROADRUNNER: Nicknamed 'George' for the Seinfeld character, there was nothing sluggish or bumbling about Jason Castagna's attack on the ball in 2017. A key member of Richmond's high-octane group of small forwards, his speed, tackling pressure and fierce attack on marking contests were central to the side's renaissance. Castagna's 26th goal of the season—an inch-perfect snap from a messy chain of hacked disposals—was an unconventional Grand Final sealer, in that it came at the 20-minute mark of the third term. With a 33-point lead at that point and after they had scored nine of the last ten goals, the Tigers were never going to loosen their grip on the Cup.

STATURE OF DAVID: In the biggest game of his career, David Astbury blanketed a variety of opponents, including Adelaide's talismanic captain Taylor Walker. Astbury kept the Crows spearhead out of the contest in the first half and contributed brilliantly to the dismantling of Adelaide's vaunted forward pack. Josh Jenkins and Andy Otten also came off second best. "We're Kings of the MCG," Astbury said after the game. "I couldn't be prouder." He also couldn't have played his role with greater diligence. Astbury's favourite film actor is Big Lebowski star John Goodman. Like Goodman, the Tiger tall's dependability allows the mercurial talents around him to shine.

STANDING TALL: When Shaun Grigg arrived at Tigerland from Carlton at the end of the 2010 AFL season, it's highly unlikely he could have foreseen a future in which he was a 190cm backup ruckman in a Premiership side, but that is just what happened in 2017. Pitching in for five-minute bursts, to give Toby Nankervis a rest, added flexibility to the Richmond line-up. Grigg added a goal to 17 possessions, making his 192nd League appearance the stuff of dreams. Statistics can't be generated to explain his calming influence on and off the field as a consistent senior player.

BUTLER SERVICE: The least heralded of the Richmond's mosquito fleet did not deviate from his season-long approach of haranguing and harassing defenders into mistakes. That pressure, chasing, tackling and bursts of energy netted him a fourth-quarter goal but, more importantly, regularly trapped the ball inside Richmond's attacking 50 and paved the way for many other scoring opportunities. For Richmond's opener, Butler might have blazed away from 40 metres out but played the percentages and ensured Josh Caddy would finish the job. The 20-year-old finished his maiden League season with 30 goals, a cherished Premiership medallion, and the club's best first-year player award.

TOUGH AS NAILS: Beloved of the Tiger Army for his infectious optimism and fearless attack on the contest, durable utility Brandon Ellis again didn't miss a game for the season. On Grand Final day he also ended his 106th consecutive appearance in the yellow and black with the medal he's always craved. Ellis thrived in 2017 by recalibrating his approach to the game. Shifting from the wing to half-back, he made an impact by rebounding strongly and guarding an impressive variety of opposition forwards as the need arose.

SPIRIT ANIMAL: All year Kane Lambert's aggressive, no-frills approach to winning the ball, defending grimly and helping out his teammates typified Richmond's dramatic reversal of fortune. His Grand Final display was no different, continuing Lambert's path as the club's most improved player. He rose to the occasion best in the second half, driving the ball into attack and kicking Richmond's seventh goal in a row to break Adelaide hearts barely 10 minutes into the third quarter—one of three majors in which he played a central role. Lambert's persistence and dedication transformed him from a VFL afterthought to third place-getter in the Jack Dyer medal in a Premiership year. A heart and soul performer.

SIREN SONG: It had been a foregone conclusion for much of the final quarter, but the reverberations of the final siren prompted sweet release for Trent Cotchin and his teammates. The Tigers skipper enjoyed a solitary moment of ecstasy before he was swamped by teammates and began the very public business of celebrating the ultimate football achievement.

MUTUAL RESPECT: Neither man could have predicted how Grand Final day would turn out, but there was mutual admiration between Damien Hardwick and Adelaide's Don Pyke. The Crows coach took on the top job amid the most emotionally difficult circumstances the club had ever faced, following the death of his predecessor Phil Walsh. Having turned Adelaide into a ladder-topping side who played attractive and engaging football, Pyke and his players earned the respect of all football fans.

TIGER TIME

PREMIERS

Once the final siren soared, there was little left to do but celebrate if you were a Tigers fan. Having collapsed on each other in delirious piles, Richmond's 22 Premiership heroes were soon wiping tears from their eyes and walking across the presentation dais for their medals. Some stared longingly at them, almost refusing to believe they were real.

Another man who'd openly wept in the closing stages of the game was Matthew Richardson, a 282-game hero of the yellow and black, and a man who strove valiantly in doomed pursuit of what Richmond's players had just achieved. Appropriately, 'Richo' had been chosen by Richmond to present the Premiership Cup, should it be won by his old side.

In scenes that will live forever in the mind's eye, a beaming Richardson strode onto the dais, handed the precious silverware to Messrs Hardwick and Cotchin, and scooted off the stage, but not before throwing both fists into the air in a moment of spontaneous joy. Richardson said later he'd just wanted to stay out of the way and let the players enjoy their moment. Yet that wouldn't have rung true. In releasing decades of pent-up emotion, instead he perfectly encapsulated the sense of unbridled joy and relief among the Tigers constituency.

SINKING IN: Not a single player in the 2017 Grand Final had played in a League decider before, and there was no escaping the dizzying novelty of posing for the first of countless celebratory team photos. Too much yellow confetti could never be enough. **Back row (L-R):** Daniel Butler, Dustin Martin, Nick Vlastuin, Shaun Grigg, Daniel Rioli, Trent Cotchin, Jack Riewoldt, Jacob Townsend, Kamdyn McIntosh, Jack Graham, Josh Caddy, Toby Nankervis. **Front row (L-R):** Dylan Grimes, David Astbury, Alex Rance, Dion Prestia, Nathan Broad, Shane Edwards, Brandon Ellis, Jason Castagna, Bachar Houli.

SWEET RELIEF: Having run themselves ragged all day, Bachar Houli and captain Trent Cotchin fall to the MCG turf in warm embrace, soon to be joined by Shane Edwards. Between them the trio had endured much heart ache in more than 500 games for the club, but on the day, their contributions went a long way towards ensuring the Tigers maintained level heads amid the chaos of Grand Final day.

FAMILY VALUES: A coach's favourite and unstoppable force all year, Dustin Martin is also—to the palpable relief of fans—now a Tiger for life. "His season ranks as the most special I've seen from a player," coach Damien Hardwick said, backing similar claims by League legend Leigh Matthews. Martin's season was, indeed, like no other. He took home the Brownlow Medal, the Norm Smith Medal, the AFLPA's MVP award, the Gary Ayres Medal (best player in the finals), and the Jack Dyer Medal, as well as a swag of media awards. But, as he noted in several interviews after the Grand Final, the only one he wanted was the Premiership Medal.

TIGER TIME

WE DID IT: Jack Riewoldt and Alex Rance were among the catalysts of the Richmond renaissance. This time the team's bookends met in the middle of the ground for once, and in the best possible circumstances. Rance had considered quitting football in 2015, but the AFL's most talented defender was rewarded for his perseverance and faith in teammates.

JUST REWARDS: No footballer epitomised the Tiger frustrations of decades gone by quite like 282-game champion Matthew Richardson, who was the perfect man to usher in Tiger celebrations. After handing over the Cup, Richo chose to exit stage right, but couldn't resist a few spontaneous air punches as he left the dais. "One thing I thought was give it to them and get off the stage and let the players enjoy it," Richardson said afterwards. "But I couldn't help myself!" Tiger fans wouldn't have wanted it any other way.

DREAMS COME TRUE: Neither man could have credibly predicted the way 2017 would turn out for Richmond, but Damien Hardwick and Trent Cotchin couldn't contain their glee at finally achieving the ultimate. Hardwick tasted Premiership success as a player with Essendon and Port Adelaide, and now joins the illustrious company of Ron Barassi, Leigh Matthews and Mick Malthouse as the only four men to have won flags at three different clubs. Cotchin clinched a treasured first.

STICKY SITUATION: As long as Gatorade exists, triumphant footballers will be pouring vats of it over the heads of their coaches, and Damien Hardwick partook in the sporting rite thanks to Dustin Martin—Dusty again perfectly hitting his target.

STORMIN' NORMAN: Dustin Martin joined fellow Richmond legends Kevin Bartlett and Maurice Rioli as a popular winner of the Norm Smith Medal, but he stands on his own among all League players in history for completing a clean sweep of every other major AFL award too—a Brownlow, a Premiership medallion, the Leigh Matthews Trophy and just about every media award on offer in a dizzying procession of trips to the stage. He is the only player in the game's history to win a Brownlow and Norm Smith in the same season.

WINNERS ARE GRINNERS: In a shot that will go straight to the pool room of every player, Richmond's Grand Final heroes sink to the MCG turf with their cherished Premiership medals and the object Richmond fans have agonised over for decades. There was no wiping the smiles off their faces at this point, and, already, many tears had been shed.

CULT HEROES: When Nick Vlastuin took his turn ferrying the Premiership Cup around the boundary, he stopped for a photo with his popular former teammate Nathan Foley. Foley was a 154-game fan favourite and Jack Dyer Medal runner-up who retired due to a degenerative knee injury at the end of the 2015 season.

DYNAMIC DUO: Jack Riewoldt gave Jacob Townsend a hug for a job well done. The easy rapport and mutual care among Richmond players in 2017 was a result of a concerted effort to open up to each other and to forge deeper personal connections. Each had his own story. Only months before Grand Final day Townsend was languishing in the VFL—where he would claim the JJ Liston medal as the feeder League's best player—and wondering whether a career in carpentry awaited him in 2017. "I was playing twos and thought I was done, my career was over," he told reporters. "To play five games all season and win a flag, I'm lost for words." The tools will need to wait a few more years yet.

PREMIERS

MASTER'S APPRENTICE: Trent Cotchin could have been forgiven for not burdening his shoulders with any more weight, but by the time victory was secured he was more than happy to chair Daniel Rioli around the ground with some precious cargo in tow. Rioli hurt his ankle late in the game—an injury that required post-season surgery.

WAR CHEST: Dustin Martin had more jewellery around his neck than Mr T once his extraordinary 2017 season was done, and given the relief of snaring the one prize he was after, could even afford a few uncharacteristic smiles for the camera. Suddenly, a life lived in the glaring spotlight seemed entirely worth it.

TIGERS OF OLD: Twenty-two lucky players experienced the exhilarating feeling of Premiership success in 2017, but they paused to acknowledge countless others who'd contributed to the cause along the way. Here Alex Rance soaks in the moment with his former defensive partner Troy Chaplin, who retired a year before the Tigers went all the way.

FEELING THE LOVE: It was hard fitting everyone in, but the celebrations soon became a whole-squad effort as both fans and the Tiger players who missed out on selection in the final 22 joined in the festivities.

SITTING PRETTY: While Kamdyn McIntosh, Nick Vlastuin and Trent Cotchin shared the moment in the company of family and supporters, Dustin Martin stood triumphant above them, with a little help from an old Tiger friend, Jake King. Sitting at home in New Zealand, Martin's father Shane was equally proud of his son's achievements.

PREMIERS

THANKS BOSS: The tears rolling down Brendon Gale's cheeks as the final siren soared were testament to the Tigers CEO's emotional investment in the club. A playing veteran of Richmond's 1995 and 2001 finals campaigns (the last of his 244 games for the Tigers was the 2001 losing Preliminary Final) now leads a sporting juggernaut with more than 75,000 diehard members and a blueprint for sustained success on and off the field. A hug from Dustin Martin and Jack Riewoldt was among the rewards for his years of hard work since taking the CEO role in 2009.

STANDING STRONG: Born in Killarney, West Virginia, Peggy O'Neal took an unconventional path into the ranks of footy administrators. In becoming not only the first female president, but the first to guide an AFL side to Premiership success, she is now cemented in Tiger history. Like most at the club, she was under siege a year earlier, weathering an off-season attempt to overthrow her Richmond board. O'Neal's reappointment of Hardwick, against vocal opposition, has now been vindicated in the grandest sense. "It's not one thing, it's a lot of people doing a lot of things," she said after the triumph.

LIFT-OFF: There were times early in the season when Trent Cotchin had to remind himself to embrace the lighter moments in life—an approach that was tested when he was in danger of missing the Grand Final after a contentious bump on Dylian Shiel in the Preliminary Final. Now the smiles can't be wiped from his face

PREMIERS

ENTOURAGE: Having spent years as the ugly ducklings of AFL football, Richmond players are all now learning to live with hordes of photographers following their every move. They ran a gauntlet of cameras before squeezing down the race and into the club's inner sanctum.

167

PREMIERS

YOUTH BEFORE BEAUTY: Newcomer Jack Graham helps his veteran skipper escort the Premiership Cup down the MCG race for the most highly-anticipated rendition of the club song.

TIGER TIME

YELLOW AND BLACK: Richmond's rousing club song was written in 1962 by popular entertainer Jack Malcolmson, at the behest of Alf Barnett, a club committeeman. When Malcolmson completed the first draft he felt like something was amiss, that a line needed to be added. Thus "yellow and black" entered the lyric sheet and club lore. Rarely has a rendition been belted out with as much gusto as Dustin Martin, Trent Cotchin and Shaun Grigg managed here. Tigers strength and conditioning coach Luke Meehan and long-time team manager Mark Opie join in the celebrations.

MR BRIGHTSIDE: Now the respected and mature leader of a youthful forward line, Jack Riewoldt in party mode is another story altogether. The Tiger hero embraced his inner rock star during the game's emotional aftermath, staying true to a pre-match promise of taking to the stage to help Brandon Flowers provide vocals for The Killers if his side got up. "The guy in yellow had a helluva night," the band later tweeted. The festivities were only just beginning.

PARTY TIME

When the novelist George Johnston wrote that Melbourne has no summer, only a period of hibernation between football seasons, he probably had a Richmond supporter in mind. The rarest breed of all fanatics, the average Tiger lifer has endured sustained periods of footballing disappointment. In weathering the club's inherent tendency towards the shambolic, you often wondered why they were still turning up, let alone barracking uproariously by their massed thousands.

For their troubles these superfans have also put up with the witless taunts of rival supporters: 'Ninth again?' 'How about that 2004 draft class?' 'When does the next five-year plan start?' 'Oh, that's so Richmondy?' This is called faith, or loyalty, or maybe madness in the face of insurmountable odds. When club CEO Brendon Gale unveiled ambitious plans for three Premierships by 2020, and 70,000 members, many doubters laughed. In fact, the Tigers are ahead of schedule. Now, when anyone mentions the number nine, it's more likely to be in the reverential tones afforded to the 2017 Premiership captain.

Tiger diehards are also impressive for their sheer biographical variety; rumpled bar fly comedian Mick Molloy; urbane TV host and columnist Waleed Aly; outspoken radio shock-jock Steve Price; introspective novelist Christos Tsiolkas; bolshy Age chief football writer Caroline Wilson. Sometimes American lawyers from Appalachian mining villages move to Melbourne and find themselves drawn immediately to the men in yellow and black—just ask Peggy O'Neal, now among an exclusive group of Richmond Premiership presidents. She stands on her own as the first woman in League history to achieve the feat.

Since 1980, what every member of the Tiger Army shared was an illogical but unshakable sense that things would turn out in the end—that sporting karma would reward them for their indefatigable chanting, those artfully-sewn duffle coat patches in honour of long-forgotten half-back flankers, all the impassioned calls to uncaring talkback radio hosts, and a basic refusal to concede there might be better ways of spending Saturday afternoons.

The triumph of 2017 is for them, as coach Damien Hardwick explained on the presentation dais. It is reward for a boisterous and loyal group of true believers who turned up, week in and week out, rain, hail or shine. According to a survey released by Roy Morgan Research during Grand Final week, only half of all Richmond supporters consider themselves religiously inclined. It's probably time they looked a little closer at their definition of devotion.

BRINGING IT HOME: There were scenes of unbridled joy when Richmond players presented the Premiership Cup to the thousands of fans who crowded inside Punt Road Oval for the club's family day. All year the Tiger Army's ranks had swelled and now they were an unstoppable force. Trent Cotchin, Damien Hardwick and Jack Riewoldt were lapping it up.

FAN'S EYE VIEW: There was a surreal but welcome sight confronting the Tigerland faithful when Trent Cotchin and Damien Hardwick put the exclamation mark on 24 hours of non-stop partying. In the areas surrounding Yarra Park, Richmond fans continued to dance in the streets. Jubilant Tigers (L-R) Jacob Townsend, Daniel Rioli, Trent Cotchin, Bachar Houli, David Astbury, Damien Hardwick, Shaun Grigg, Dustin Martin, Jack Riewoldt and Dion Prestia soak it all in.

TRIBAL LAW: Tiger fans poured into Punt Road Oval in the hope of joining in the Premiership celebrations, spilling from every vantage point inside the club's traditional home and trying to catch a glimpse of Damien Hardwick's men.

TIGER TIME

TROOPING THE COLOUR: As well as being the loudest supporters in the competition, Richmond's diehard fans are some of the best dressed.

WAR PAINT: It's likely there was a national shortage of yellow and black face paint in the final week of September, with fans spending hours working on their Tigeriffic creations. At the Grand Final parade, visiting Adelaide fans were confronted by a veritable army of Richmond supporters.

PARTY TIME

WHO'S THE BOSS?: In 2017 Danielle Hardwick was recognised by Tiger fans as the hidden genius behind her husband's growing success. "You're not the man I married," she had told the Tigers coach at one point during the club's 2016 implosion, and having resolved to rediscover his happy-go-lucky side, Mr Hardwick was on his way to being named the AFL Coaches Association coach of the year.

TRUE BELIEVERS: The Tigers' fairytale season was just reward for fans who'd endured every false dawn and multiple crises since Richmond last ruled the football world. Nobody could accuse the Tiger Army of being bandwagon fans—they'd been there through thick and thin.

TIGER ROAR: Club legend Matthew Richardson acted on behalf of the Richmond faithful when he let his emotions run wild in the wake of the Tiger triumph. Nobody could begrudge the club legend this moment of exultation.

TIGER TIME

PEOPLE POWER: Jack Riewoldt gives the Tiger faithful what they've been longing for, climbing onto the MCG fence and hoisting the Premiership Cup into the twilight air. Richmond defender Nathan Broad looks on.

BY THE NUMBERS

1
Norm Smith Medallist:
Dustin Martin

1
Brownlow Medallist:
Dustin Martin

1
Jack Dyer Medallist:
Dustin Martin

2
All Australians:
Dustin Martin and Alex Rance

4
The number of single-digit losing margins the Tigers suffered in 2017—three of them under a kick in consecutive weeks between rounds seven and nine

5
The number of games it took first-year player Jack Graham to win his first Premiership

11
The number of Premierships Richmond has now won

13
The ladder position from which no other club had climbed from the previous season to be crowned Premiers

16
The number of years Tigers fans had waited for a Finals victory.

18
Richmond wins during the 2017 season

37
The number of years since Richmond won their last Premiership

38
The number of senior players used by Richmond for the season

48
Points: the winning margin on Grand Final day

54
Goals kicked for the season by Jack Riewoldt, his eighth half-century haul in the last nine seasons

150
The number of Inside-50s Dustin Martin managed in 2017—a league-leading total

242
The number of one-percenters committed by Alex Rance, the most of any AFL player

744
Dustin Martin's disposal count in 25 appearances in 2017—363 of them were contested.

75,777
The number of paid-up Richmond members by Grand Final day

100,021
The number of fans who attended on AFL Grand Final day

8.4
Million Australians watched Richmond's Premiership triumph on TV, accoding to Roy Morgan Research

RICHMOND
EST 1885

The Slattery Media Group,
Level 39/385 Bourke Street, Melbourne, Victoria, 3000.

First published by The Slattery Media Group, 2017.
Re-printed, 2017
Text copyright © The Slattery Media Group.

All rights reserved. No part of this publication may be reproduced, stored in a retrieval system or transmitted in any form by any means without the prior permission of the copyright owner. Inquiries should be made to the publisher.

Images Copyright © Australian Football League, 2017.
Used with permission.

®™ The AFL logo and competing team logos, emblems and names used are all trademarks of and used under licence from the owner, the Australian Football League, by whom all copyright and other rights of reproduction are reserved. Australian Football League, AFL House, 140 Harbour Esplanade, Docklands, Victoria, Australia, 3008.

Prints of photos published in *Tiger Time* can be purchased at aflphotos.com.au.

The publisher wishes to thank the Richmond Football Club for its support with this publication.

 A catalogue record for this book is available from the National Library of Australia

Group Publisher: Geoff Slattery
Editor: Geoff Slattery
Writer: Russell Jackson
Designers: Kate Slattery & Anthony Costa

Printed by Mercedes Waratah, Melbourne.

www.slatterymedia.com